Endorse

"Christia... ... ... very real questions. How does Scripture structure a church, order worship, organize ministry, and define biblical leadership? Those are just examples of the questions that are answered clearly, carefully, and winsomely in this new series from 9Marks. I am so thankful for this ministry and for its incredibly healthy and hopeful influence in so many faithful churches. I eagerly commend this series."

R. Albert Mohler Jr., President, The Southern Baptist Theological Seminary

"Sincere questions deserve thoughtful answers. If you're not sure where to start in answering these questions, let this series serve as a diving board into the pool. These minibooks are winsomely to-the-point and great to read together with one friend or one hundred friends."

Gloria Furman, author, *Missional Motherhood* and *The Pastor's Wife*

"As a pastor, I get asked lots of questions. I'm approached by unbelievers seeking to understand the gospel, new believers unsure about next steps, and maturing believers wanting help answering questions from their Christian family, friends, neighbors, or coworkers. It's in these moments that I wish I had a book to give them that was brief, answered their questions, and pointed them in the right direction for further study. Church Questions is a series that provides just that. Each booklet tackles one question in a biblical, brief, and practical manner. The series may be called Church Questions, but it could be called 'Church Answers.' I intend to pick these up by the dozens and give them away regularly. You should too."

Juan R. Sanchez, Senior Pastor, High Pointe
Baptist Church, Austin, Texas

"Where can we Christians find reliable answers to our common questions about life together at church—without having to plow through long, expensive books? The Church Questions booklets meet our need with answers that are biblical, thoughtful, and practical. For pastors, this series will prove a trustworthy resource for guiding church members toward deeper wisdom and stronger unity."

Ray Ortlund, President, Renewal Ministries

How Can
Women Thrive in
the Local Church?

Church Questions

How Can Women Thrive in the Local Church?

Keri Folmar

WHEATON, ILLINOIS

How Can Women Thrive in the Local Church?

Copyright © 2021 by 9Marks

Published by Crossway
        1300 Crescent Street
        Wheaton, Illinois 60187

Cover design: Jordan Singer

First printing 2021

Printed in the United States of America

Trade paperback ISBN: 978-1-4335-7219-7
ePub ISBN: 978-1-4335-7222-7
PDF ISBN: 978-1-4335-7220-3
Mobipocket ISBN: 978-1-4335-7221-0

Library of Congress Cataloging-in-Publication Data

Names: Folmar, Keri, author.
Title: How can women thrive in the local church? / Keri Folmar.
Description: Wheaton, Illinois : Crossway, 2021. | Series: Church questions | Includes bibliographical references and index.
Identifiers: LCCN 2020028967 (print) | LCCN 2020028968 (ebook) | ISBN 9781433572197 (trade paperback) | ISBN 9781433572203 (pdf) | ISBN 9781433572210 (mobipocket) | ISBN 9781433572227 (epub)
Subjects: LCSH: Women in Christianity.
Classification: LCC BV639.W7 F65 2021 (print) | LCC BV639.W7 (ebook) | DDC 253.082—dc23
LC record available at https://lccn.loc.gov/2020028967
LC ebook record available at https://lccn.loc.gov/2020028968

Crossway is a publishing ministry of Good News Publishers.

BP		30	29	28	27	26	25	24	23	22	21
15	14	13	12	11	10	9	8	7	6	5	4	3	2

For the body does not consist of one member but of many. If the foot should say, "Because I am not a hand, I do not belong to the body," that would not make it any less a part of the body. And if the ear should say, "Because I am not an eye, I do not belong to the body," that would not make it any less a part of the body. If the whole body were an eye, where would be the sense of hearing? If the whole body were an ear, where would be the sense of smell? But as it is, God arranged the members in the body, each one of them, as he chose. If all were a single member, where would the body be? As it is, there are many parts, yet one body.

1 Corinthians 12:14–20

Are you thriving at your church? After years of discipling and counseling sisters in the church, I've seen a number of women struggle to find their place and spiritually thrive. My friend Joan happily attended women's Bible study but was too busy on the weekends to attend church.[1]Ashley found it hard to meet new people and felt like an outsider in our congregation. Natasha was hurt because she didn't think her gifts and talents were being adequately used and wondered how she could participate in church ministry.

Do you find yourself in any of those situations? Are you struggling to thrive in your church?

As women, we have unique ways that we get to display God's glory. Being a woman is a gift, a stewardship from God. We are essential and indispensable to God's kingdom. But being a woman also comes with unique challenges. With busy lives, pulled this-way-and-that by responsibilities at school or work or home, how can we flourish spiritually?

If you resonate with the previous paragraphs, this booklet is for you. My goal is to encourage you to enjoy the fullness of God's grace available for you in the gospel and experience this joy in meaningful, life-giving relationships with the people of God in a local church. I want you to thrive. In fact, as I'll explain below, you can't separate those two things. We simply *can't* thrive spiritually apart from the church.

I'm sure your church isn't perfect—it's made up of sinners saved only by grace—but it is a beautiful display of God's glory. Just think about your brothers and sisters in the church. Consider that brother God saved from a futile life of career idolatry. Consider that sister he saved from chasing after elusive love in worldly relationships. In story after story like these, the lesson is plain: "Through the church the manifold wisdom of God [is] made known to the rulers and authorities in the heavenly places" (Eph. 3:10). In saving people from a diversity of backgrounds by the gospel of his Son, God showcases his wisdom not only for the world to see but for all the heavenly hosts to marvel at. The church is God's vehicle for his glory, and it's our destination if we want to spiritually thrive.

Sisters, here are eight essentials for thriving in the church.

1. You Must Be Alive in Christ

Julia grew up in the church. Like other kids with godly Christian parents, she faithfully attended church, was part of the youth group, and even attended church camp every summer. When she went to college, she found a church that reminded her of home, but her attendance quickly became sporadic. As an honors student with a full load of classes, she began to spend her weekends blowing off steam at parties. Church just wasn't as exciting as all the new experiences college offered—and besides, after a few days of partying, she needed Sunday mornings to catch up on sleep.

A Christian friend noticed the contrast between Julia's claim to be a Christian and the way she lived her life. This friend invited her to a church that taught the Bible and clearly proclaimed the gospel. At first, Julia was bored with the sermons, but then the Word of God started to convict her and shape the way she thought about her life. Over time, she realized that while she labeled herself a Christian, she didn't really know the God of the Bible. After conversations with her friends and the pastor, she repented and put her trust in Jesus.

From that moment, church life changed for Julia. It was no longer a social club where she could meet friends and be entertained. It was a necessity. She needed the preaching of God's word like she needed food. She longed for fellowship like she thirsted for water. Julia was baptized, became a member, and even moved into a house with other single women from the church. Her life began to revolve around the church—she began to thrive.

Jesus said, "I am the vine; you are the branches" (John 15:5). He told his disciples, "If anyone does not abide in me he is thrown away like a branch and withers; and the branches are gathered, thrown into the fire, and burned" (v. 6). Jesus is the vine from which the church grows. We receive our sustenance from him. If you're not attached to the vine, you're not receiving spiritual nourishment. In other words, you're not alive. Eventually you'll wither up and be destroyed. But if you're attached to the vine, you'll flourish along with the other branches. Jesus promises, "Whoever abides in me and I in him, he it is that bears much fruit, for apart from me you can do nothing" (v. 5).

Jesus died so that we could live in him. God created men and women to glorify him and enjoy him forever. But beginning with Adam and Eve, all throughout human history mankind has rejected God, breaking relationship with him and ruining themselves. Although we were created for God's glory, we "all have sinned and fall short" of that glory (Rom. 3:23). The Bible tells us that "the wages of sin is death" (Rom. 6:23), but God sent his beloved Son to pay the wages for us. Jesus went to the cross and died for the sins of anyone who would repent and believe. And God raised him from the dead in triumph over sin and death. Jesus Christ "gave himself for us to redeem us from all lawlessness and to purify for himself a people for his own possession" (Titus 2:14). Those people are the church. If we are attached to Jesus, the vine, we are attached to the church.

Are you having a hard time getting up on Sunday morning? Are you bored with the sermons and apathetic about fellowship with the saints? Are you languishing in your local church? "Examine yourselves, to see whether you are in the faith" (2 Cor. 13:5). You have to be alive to thrive. It could be that you're not thriving because you're not really alive.

2. Join a Local Church

I grew up attending a variety of churches in different denominations. My father wasn't a

Christian, but my mother had grown up going to church, so she would choose a church in a convenient location, and we would attend sporadically.

After becoming a Christian, I followed the same pattern. I would attend whatever church suited me best in the moment. The sermons often provided a spiritual pick-me-up, and the programs provided opportunities for friendship with other folks in my season of life. I was regularly in church, but I never thought about committing to one. I was a consumer.

Eventually, I started attending a church where the pastor systematically preached through books of the Bible. He didn't just use the Bible to talk about his own ideas or try to inspire me spiritually. The point of the biblical text was the point of his sermon. I also noticed something intriguing about the church's culture. The people were unusually committed to gathering together and to loving one another. I began to attend on Sunday mornings, Sunday evenings, and Wednesday nights and was regularly greeted by the same people.

One Sunday evening, as I was saying good-bye to the pastor at the door of the church, he said, "Keri, you've been coming to this church for three months. Why don't you become a member?" I had no problem with membership. It had just never occurred to me that *I* should join a church. I attended a membership class, went through an interview with the pastor, and joined.

Being a member of that church changed my life. I didn't just attend church anymore; I was *part* of it. It was *my* church. Those people were committed to me, and I was committed to them. They were *my* brothers and sisters. Even more, I was developing relationships with everyone in the church, not just a small group of them who were my age and stage of life. Soon my calendar was brimming with meetings with older saints, married couples, parents of young children, single people, and widows. They were praying for me, rooting for me, spending time with me, looking out for me. They were family—one even became my husband!

The Bible doesn't have a category for solo Christians: "You are fellow citizens with the saints and members of the household of God, built on the foundation of the apostles and prophets, Christ Jesus himself being the cornerstone, in whom the whole structure, being joined together, grows into a holy temple in the Lord" (Eph. 2:19–21). Jesus is the rock that holds everything together. The apostles and prophets (the Scriptures) are the foundation. But the structure is made up of stones "joined together," "members of a household." The church is made up of people who are cemented to one another. You and your fellow church members "are being built together into a dwelling place for God by the Spirit" (v. 22). Don't you want to be a part of that house?

Of course, don't just join any church. Join a healthy church, one that rightly preaches the gospel and values church membership. Join a church like the ones we see in the book of Acts: "those who received his word were baptized, ... And they devoted themselves to the apostles' teaching and the fellowship, to the breaking of bread and the prayers" (Acts 2:41–42). This passage is the New Testament's pattern for the church.

Baptism, upon profession of faith, is the entry-gate into the church. Devotion to the Scriptures, fellowship, and prayer characterize the church. And the Lord's Supper ("the breaking of bread") is how the church corporately confesses its faith in Christ and their commitment to one another. These elements are what you should look for in a local church.

If you're a member of a biblical church, you will be in a position to spiritually thrive. The New Testament highlights this point by regularly describing Christians as members of a body—a local church. An arm or a leg won't thrive if it's disconnected from the body. So also you can't thrive spiritually as a Christian if you're not a committed member of a local church. As Paul writes, the body of Christ "builds itself up in love" when "each part is working properly" (Eph. 4:16). Do you want to thrive spiritually? You need to be built up by the body of Christ.

I can look back on my Christian life and identify remarkable times of spiritual growth: attending camp as a teenager, cutting off worldly ties after college, dealing with physical suffering as a young adult, and enjoying fellowship with close Christian friends. These were fruitful times. But nothing supercharged my growth as a Christian like joining a local church. As a church member, I was taught the word of God by other members who cared for my spiritual health, encouraged me to love the Lord in my personal and professional life, prodded me to serve in ways that weren't always comfortable, and challenged me to share the gospel widely.

I'm no longer a member of the church I first joined because I've moved away. But I've been a member of a church in every place I've lived since, and as I look back, I can see God's kindness in every church I've joined. Commitment to my local church has turned a life of drastic ups and downs into one of steady growth in the right direction. Daily, my brothers and sisters have built me up in love as we have pursued Christ together and cared for one another's spiritual well-being.

If you want to thrive spiritually, join a church.

3. Prioritize the Weekly Gathering

Over the past fifteen years, I've had the privilege of observing and caring for members of my church. From my pastor's wife birds-eye view, I've witnessed all types of difficulties and struggles that keep women on the outskirts of church life: unbelieving husbands, rebellious teenagers, kids' activities or sports, singleness, widowhood, and countless others. But church isn't just a place to tinker around the edges; we need to dig in. And to do that, we must prioritize the weekly gathering.

The word "church" actually means "assembly." It's an assembly of men and women gathered together to sing to one another, pray together, sit together under God's word, and observe the ordinances of baptism and the Lord's Supper. As we saw in Acts, Jesus's church has been doing these things from the very beginning. When we gather, the Lord is among us in a particular and special way (Matt. 18:20). He uses this time to show us his excellencies and mold us together into a people who become like him.

How does this shaping take place?

> Let us consider how to stir up one another
> to love and good works, not neglecting to
> meet together, as is the habit of some, but
> encouraging one another, and all the more
> as you see the Day drawing near. (Heb.
> 10:24–25)

On Sundays, we motivate one another to love
and good works by letting "the word of Christ
dwell in [us] richly, teaching and admonishing
one another in all wisdom, singing psalms and
hymns and spiritual songs, with thankfulness in
[our] hearts to God" (Col. 3:16). Do you feel the
sense of urgency the New Testament puts on our
weekly gathering? We help others persevere on
the long road of obedience by consistently gathering together. We sing, not just for ourselves,
but to enliven the faith of others. As we sit under
God's word, we commit to helping one another
follow that word together. When we gather, we're
a picture of heaven that encourages us to remain
faithful as we wait for Christ's return.

Perhaps you have some favorite preachers whom you enjoy watching on YouTube or listening to online. I have mine, and I regularly listen to their sermons. They often help my heart and refocus my mind on the things of God. But I can't live off online preaching. If I stay home and neglect to gather with the church, I can't look up and join Etienne, who's joyfully leading songs. I can't look over and be encouraged by Anna with her head raised, singing exuberantly. My heart won't leap in thankfulness as I see Narmada, who a year ago didn't know the Lord, lock arms with another sister as they worship our good God.

Similarly, if I don't sit under the same preaching with my brothers and sisters in my local church, I won't have the delight of discussing the sermon with them. I'll miss out on the accountability of applying it to our lives together. We are a community, an outpost of heaven, shaped by the word of God we hear together. Our shared Sunday morning experience shapes our life together. It gives us language to encourage one another and helps us all walk the same walk. We're committed to each other. Collectively hearing the preached word encourages us, increases our love for one another, and stirs our hearts to do good.

Prioritizing the weekly gathering not only builds up the church, it also impacts those who watch from the outside. Consider the message you send to unbelievers if you don't prioritize gathering with God's people. Do you have an unbelieving husband or rebellious children you want to come to know the Lord? Do kids' soccer games or school parties keep you from gathering with God's people? If you stay home from church because of unbelieving family, you're telling your family they're more important than God.

Worship is about value—we worship what we value most. If your family is of more value to you than your God, then you're worshiping them. Why would they want to worship a God who is beneath them? Conversely, if you prioritize the gathering on the first day of the week, you make a compelling statement that God is worthy to be worshiped, that he's your highest value, and that you need and enjoy him and his people. This is a God your family can worship!

So, by all means, cheerfully drag those rebellious children with you to church, even if they're teenagers. Make it non-negotiable. Sports or birthday parties shouldn't trump God and his people. Show them by your enthusiastic commitment that true life centers on the one true God. Don't underestimate godly examples for your teenagers. We're indebted to the college students and twenty-somethings who sit up front in our church, showing our children what it means for young people to follow the Lord.

Perhaps it's not family keeping you from church, but your singleness. If you're a single woman or a widow, it can be hard to go to church alone. But consider Dorcas in Acts 9:36–41. Peter raised this precious widow from the dead because she was so beloved by the church. Reflect on how Paul valued singleness. He wrote, "To the unmarried and the widows I say that it is good for them to remain single, as I am" (1 Cor. 7:8). Why? Because "the unmarried or betrothed woman is anxious about the things of the Lord, how to be holy in body and spirit. But the married woman is anxious about worldly things, how to please her husband" (1 Cor. 7:34). The undivided devotion of single women and widows are huge blessings to the church.

Our friend Elizabeth was a single woman in her late twenties who was close with many other women and families in our church. She was also interested in missions. So when we announced we were moving to Dubai, she volunteered to quit her job and go along with us to take care of our kids while we were settling in. A month turned into a year during which Elizabeth joined our new church, worked with youth, shared the gospel with many Muslims, and encouraged numerous women. Her warm smile and enthusiastic greetings stirred up many to love and good works. She used her singleness to build up the church.

Both singleness and marriage come with unique challenges. But don't let your life circumstances keep you from God's people. Are you regularly gathering with your local church, letting "the word of Christ dwell in you richly"

(Col. 3:16)? Don't let difficult situations hold you back. Prioritize the weekly gathering and thrive.

4. Sit More Than You Serve

Some women are servant-hearted by nature. They're making meals, taking care of children, helping in the office, and greeting people at the front door. What would the church do without these dear women? But sometimes we women get so caught up in serving that we never have time to sit. Service is part of spiritual growth, but it's not the primary means of growth as a Christian. The word of God is (Luke 10:38–42).

The word of God works in believers by the power of the Holy Spirit, imparting the knowledge of God and transforming us to look more like his Son, our Lord Jesus Christ. God implants his word in us (James 1:21) and uses preaching to exhort us. The Apostle Paul thanks God for the Thessalonians who received the word they heard, "not as the word of men but as what it really is, the word of God, which is at work in you believers" (1 Thess. 2:13). If your pastor preaches the Bible, not to scratch itching ears but to faithfully proclaim the message of the passage, then he is speaking the very words of God to you, and they will work in you. If you want to thrive, make sure to sit regularly under the preaching of God's word.

Take *every* advantage of the preaching and teaching ministries at your church. My dear friend Karen had a high-powered job in a presidential administration and was also a happy member of her local church. She would faithfully go to church each Sunday morning, spend time with fellow church members, and then rest at home the remainder of the day. Often, she would go out for a walk around the neighborhood and would see others going back to church for the evening service. She thought nothing of it until a friend urged her to go. Though she was tired, she went back to the church that evening. At the service she felt a mixture of dismay and encouragement. By neglecting that evening service for the better part of a year, she had missed out on sweet, enriching time with her church family. The singing was joyful and robust. They prayed about the ministry going on in the neighborhood and members' workplaces. The church also received another short sermon that applied biblical truth to her heart. Never again, she thought, would she rest her body to the neglect of restoring her soul. She became a regular at those Sunday evening services too.

Does your church have a Sunday evening service? Make time to go. Does it have a church-wide Bible study? Participate. Are periodic weekend conferences or women's retreats offered? Use these times to sit under teaching and deepen your knowledge of God's word.

In fact, use every opportunity to receive instruction from God's word. Interact with your pastors after they preach. Ask them follow-up questions. Tell them if there's something you don't understand or with which you disagree. Wrestle with the preached word and apply it to your life. Be like the Bereans who "received the word with all eagerness" and examined "the

Scriptures daily" to see if what Paul taught them was true (Acts 17:11).

Of course, you can't be like the Bereans if you only pick up your Bible on Sundays. To thrive in your local church, commit yourself to daily personal time sitting under Scripture. Second Timothy 3:16–17 is a sweeping statement about the Bible:

> All Scripture is breathed out by God and profitable for teaching, for reproof, for correction, and for training in righteousness, that the man [and woman] of God may be complete, equipped for every good work.

The words "breathed out" tell us that all of Scripture is God speaking to us. His words are all "profitable." They teach and train and reprove and correct us with the end goal of making us "complete, equipped for every good work." This means Scripture fully equips us to do everything the Lord has for us.

Do you want to be more complete and equipped? Do you want to excel in good works? Go to the Scriptures. Dig into them every day. Think them through. Let them teach you sound doctrine and train you in righteous living. Let them reprove your wrong beliefs and correct you when you sin. There's no place for intermittent fasting when it comes to the Bible. Saturate yourself with God's word.

And then, once you've absorbed God's word, fellowship with other believers and tell them what you've been learning. Ask them what the Lord has been teaching them from Scripture. In the local church, we learn God's word not just from the pastors, but from other brothers and sisters who love Jesus and his word. Open your life up to your brothers and sisters and learn what the Lord is teaching them.

The church is a place where we should serve in a variety of ways. But we should prioritize sitting under the preaching of God's word and sitting at the feet of Jesus in our own devotional times for the power we need to serve. God's word feeds our hearts so we can thrive.

5. Embrace the Church as Family and Be a Mother and a Sister

My husband and I moved from America to Dubai with our three young children for my husband to pastor a church made up of people from across the world—sixty different nations. Most of them don't look like us, speak like us, or eat like us. We come from very different cultures and certainly don't look like we're related. But we have the same Savior, and we've been repeatedly struck by the family-like bonds that we share with one another.

This family bond shows itself in innumerable ways. Nora bakes and decorates beautiful cakes for church members who get married and has done the same for each of our children's high school graduations. Wesley lived with us after he graduated from college. Tess and Ewald put up curtains in our house. Darlene and Joy have been like grandparents to our children, loving and praying for them. The church elders are genuine brothers to my husband John. I have sisters of all ages with whom I share my life.

This shouldn't surprise us. After all, Jesus promised his followers a family:

> Truly, I say to you, there is no one who has left house or brothers or sisters or mother or father or children or lands, for my sake and for the gospel, who will not receive a hundredfold now in this time, houses and brothers and sisters and mothers and children and lands, with persecutions, and in the age to come eternal life. (Mark 10:29–30)

The church is made up of the brothers, sisters, mothers, and children Jesus promised. We're adopted into this family by being united to Christ. God becomes our Father and those who believe are "brother and sister and mother" to us through Christ. Blood relatives are patterns that point us to our true and eternal family, the church.

One of the wonderful things about families is that we're not all the same. Mothers, fathers, sisters, and brothers have different parts to play and benefit one another in different ways. Fathers lead the family, and mothers come alongside the fathers to teach and train the children. The Bible doesn't have specific commands to blood sisters and brothers, but we instinctively know that sisters provide something different to a family than brothers do. I have two daughters and a son. They all confide in one another, but my daughters have longer more drawn out conversations and can relate to one another in a way my son can't. So, too, they provide him with sisterly care and advice. In other words, we all need both brothers and sisters to help us grow into maturity. For you, then, thriving in the local church means embracing being a daughter to some, a sister to others, and a mother to still others.

In the family of the church, leaders are called the elders or pastors. The two terms mean the same thing. Pastors serve as models for us and exercise authority over us through the ministry of the word. They model the Christian life by being "hospitable, a lover of good, self-controlled, upright, holy, and disciplined" (Titus 1:8). These men are responsible to "hold firm to the trust-worthy word as taught, so that [they] may be able to give instruction in sound doctrine and also to rebuke those who contradict it" (Titus 1:9). Observe them. Ask them questions. Get to know them and their families. Pray for them as they pray for you. And accept their authority over you.

How does that last line sit with you? In this era of #MeToo, some women tend to cringe when they think of men with authority. But a pastor's authority isn't abusive or power-hungry. In fact, if your pastors are abusive or power-hungry, then you should seek help, leave your church immediately, and find a different church. True pastors "care for the church of God" (Acts 20:28) through faithful Bible teaching and their own example. A pastor's authority begins and ends with Scripture. His job is to nourish the flock with God's word and to protect the church by teaching truth.

We should check all teaching by the Bible, but we should not approach our pastors with suspicion and critical spirits. In fact, Hebrews 13:17 says quite the opposite:

> Obey your leaders and submit to them, for they are keeping watch over your souls, as those who will have to give an account. Let them do this with joy and not with groaning, for that would be of no advantage to you.

Your happy submission to elder authority will be to your own advantage. You will thrive, and your elders will serve you and the church body with joy.

Intentional relationships with other women in the church will also be to your advantage. Aside from my relationship with my husband, the church-family relationships that are most precious to me are with women who are daughters, sisters, and mothers to me. My husband is a wonderful shepherd to me, but my sisters in Christ encourage me in ways that husbands just aren't designed to. When my daughters had lice, three mother-sisters in the church advised me, brought me meals and prayed for me while I spent hours combing out my daughters' hair. I have several sisters who transparently share their burdens of sin with me as I share mine, so we can keep each other accountable. And what a joy it has been to help daughter-sisters persevere through trials and come out trusting God more. (Married women, in particular, don't neglect your women friends!)

Paul reserves a special responsibility for older women—the spiritual mothers in our churches. He urges Titus to teach them "to be reverent in behavior, not slanderers or slaves to much wine" (2:3). In other words, don't be busybodies who are worldly and obsessed with entertainment. Instead, older women "are to teach what is good, and so train the young women to love their husbands and children, to be self-controlled, pure, working at home, kind, and submissive to their own husbands, that the word of God may not be reviled" (vv. 3–5). These verses aren't just about older women befriending younger women in the church. They're not primarily about teaching young women how to cook healthy meals or discipline an unruly child, although those things can be included. Titus 2:3–5 is about sharing our lives with one another: older women spending time with younger women, intentionally discipling them to live for God's glory.

When I think about women in my own church who model meaningful relationships with other women, my friend Carrie often comes to mind. Carrie became a Christian while going through a divorce. She had two young children and had never been exposed to genuine Christians until Bronwyn, another sister at my church, opened her life to Carrie. Bronwyn showed Carrie what it meant to be a Christian wife and mother. She'd regularly invite Carrie to her home and point her to a God who cares for the brokenhearted.

Then Kim came into Carrie's life too. Kim met many of Carrie's practical needs—caring for her children and helping her navigate financial obligations—and she helped her learn how to read the Bible and entrust herself to God as she suffered. Carrie learned to live the

Christian life through sisters in her church who lived it with her. Years later, Carrie then passed that same love and those same spiritual lessons to two other women in my church: Jenia and Crina.

Similarly, my friend Ranjini is fifty-something and has been a Christian a long time. She's involved in ministry and a passionate evangelist. Always engaged in Christian work, Ranjini has come to understand the centrality of the local church in the Christian life. She now regularly teaches and trains women for ministry in our congregation. She continues to reach unbelievers with the gospel, but she also meets regularly with other women in our church to read the Bible or a book on Christian living together. In addition to scheduled discipling meetings, she's a go-to woman for advice ranging from relationships to the interpretation of a passage of Scripture. There are numerous young women who consider her their Titus-2 mentor.

Paul gives no specific age limits for the older or younger woman. If you want to thrive in your local church, strive to be both. Have a network of relationships where you are discipling and are being discipled. Ask the Ranjinis at your church how to be content as a single woman, or if you're married, how to love your husband well. Reach out to the Carries in your church and teach them how to renew their minds with Scripture. With a Titus-2 focus, you will find relationships that bring you rich joy and prepare you for eternity with Christ's bride.[2]

In the church, we must love one another with brotherly love from the heart (1 Pet. 1:22), participating in the same Spirit, "in full accord and of one mind"—the mind of Christ (Phil. 2:2). The church is a family united in Christ Jesus with elders, mothers, brothers, and sisters. Are you treating your church like a club that you frequent on the weekends, or are you a mother, sister, and daughter, rooted into the relationships of a family? That family will help you thrive.

6. Don't Let Conflict or Bitterness Fester

Conflict arises in every family. In the church, if we're rubbing shoulders enough, we'll likely, on occasion, rub each other the wrong way. But we can't thrive if we allow conflict to fester.

If anyone knew about conflict it was David, the king of Israel. Second Samuel tells us that David's family was torn apart by bitterness and conflict. One of David's sons raped a half-sister (a daughter of David). Another brother avenged the sister and killed the rapist brother. That same avenging son then tried to usurp the throne and for a time forced David into exile. These were just *some* of the problems in David's family.

David knew the joy of family unity and the sorrow caused by conflict and disunity. His family conflict surely stands behind David's cry in Psalm 133:

> Behold, how good and pleasant it is
>   when brothers dwell in unity!
> It is like the precious oil on the head, ...
> It is like the dew of Hermon,
>   which falls on the mountains of Zion!
> For there the LORD has commanded the
>   blessing,
>   life forevermore.

In a three-verse psalm David praises unity among brothers and compares it to water that leads to the blessing of eternal life. Now that's thriving!

The blessing of unity is why Paul repeatedly tells churches to avoid rivalry, dissensions, and divisions. He calls these unity-destroyers the works of the flesh and lists them along with sins such as sexual immorality, sorcery, and orgies (Gal. 5:19–21). He warns, "If you bite and devour one another, watch out that you are not consumed by one another" (Gal. 5:15).

Elsewhere, Paul urges, "Do nothing from selfish ambition or conceit, but in humility count others more significant than yourselves. Let each of you look not only to his own interests, but also to the interests of others" (Phil. 2:3–4). Rivalries, jealousy, dissensions, and divisions are incompatible with the church. They can spread and grow. But we are one body with Jesus as our head. We should celebrate our different giftings and rejoice when others prosper. We should listen, speak the truth, and build each other up in love. We should emulate

Jesus, who for our interest went all the way to the cross.

Is there a woman in your church who rubs you the wrong way? Maybe she speaks too directly and leaves you feeling a little insecure. Maybe she's too indirect, and you never quite know what her comments mean. Is there a woman with whom you constantly compare yourself? Do you envy her style, abilities, gifts, family, children, or Instagram account? When you look at her life, do you think you fall short? Is there an elder in your church whom you perceive as too harsh? Have you been hurt by things that have been said or left unsaid? Sisters, don't let bitterness fester. We need to confess our sins to the Lord and to one another. We need to pursue reconciliation with brothers and sisters, even if they're unaware of the ways they've hurt us.

The Bible highlights the faith of many humble and godly women whom God used powerfully in redemptive history. But the Bible also mentions by name two women who were not known for their faith but for their divisiveness. Paul addressed these women in Philippians 4:2:

"I entreat Euodia and I entreat Syntyche to agree in the Lord." Could you imagine getting called out publicly by the Apostle Paul? After all, this letter was addressed to the whole church (Phil. 1:1)!

Sisters, if you have a disagreement or an uncomfortable relationship, do what you can to make it right. You may not be able to fix someone else's heart, but you can by the power of the Holy Spirit work on yours.

> Let all bitterness and wrath and anger and clamor and slander be put away from you, along with all malice. Be kind to one another, tenderhearted, forgiving one another, as God in Christ forgave you. (Eph. 4:31–32)

Putting away your anger and forgiving others will enable you to thrive.

7. Look for Needs and Meet Them

If you ask a career coach how to thrive at your job, she'll likely advise you to play to your strengths, downplay your weaknesses, and, above all, follow your passions. Many Christians think about spiritual gifts in the church in much the same way.

Spiritual gift inventories are readily available online. They read a lot like personality tests, but instead of finding out you're a 2 or 5 on the Enneagram, you find out if you should be doing acts of mercy or hospitality or exercising one of the other dozen-or-so spiritual gifts set out in Scripture. The assumption behind these inventories is that you can find the ministry which best fits your passions and interests, the one that will lead to your greatest spiritual fulfillment. In fact, I saw one website advertise: "Discovering and exercising your God-given spiritual gifts allows you to experience maximum fulfillment with minimum frustration in your Christian life and ministry."[3]

Wow! "Maximum fulfillment with minimum frustration." Who doesn't want that? The problem with this sort of advice is that it's all about *us*! It turns Christian life and ministry into vehicles for self-fulfillment. But this kind of self-focus makes us, and everyone around us, miserable. If my goal is me, then God help the people who get in my way.

The truth is that denying ourselves and focusing on the cause of Christ ultimately leads to fulfillment. The Holy Spirit gives us gifts not for ourselves but for glorifying God by serving others in the church.

> As each has received a gift, use it to serve one another, as good stewards of God's varied grace . . . in order that in everything God may be glorified through Jesus Christ. (1 Pet. 4:10–11)

Paul also makes this point, "To each is given the manifestation of the Spirit for the *common good*" (1 Cor. 12:7). Our focus in the church shouldn't be determining our particular gifts but determining the needs of the body. How can I serve my brothers and sisters in Christ? What can I do for the common good? We shouldn't ask how the church can platform our gifts. We should ask how we can use our gifts according to the needs of the church.[4]

When I was a single woman in my late twenties, I was asked to serve in the church nursery. As someone who spent my days working for a congressional committee on Capitol Hill, ministry to young children wasn't exactly my thing. Not only was I not gifted in it, I didn't even know how to change a diaper. But I knew I didn't have a legitimate excuse to decline, so I agreed to be put on the roster. It turns out it wasn't that difficult, and now I have sweet memories of doing puzzles with toddlers and watching one little boy enjoy riding a big yellow duck! In these moments, I wasn't merely caring for a few young children; I was enabling moms and dads to enjoy the church gathering without distraction. And, oh, how thankful I am to others who helped me in similar ways when I was raising my own three children later in my life. An hour and a half of uninterrupted corporate worship is invaluable to the mom of an infant or toddler.

One more thing: we shouldn't compare ourselves to other women in the church. Each of us has different gifts and abilities. Each of us has varying levels of margin in our life. Some of us simply have less bandwidth than others. Don't compare your gifts or service to others, especially to those who are in a different season of life. Instead, focus on what the Lord has called you to do in your particular season.

Serving others for the common good isn't always comfortable. But ultimately, we find life in denying ourselves and meeting others' needs. We thrive when we find needs and meet them.

8. Bring the Church Home

In Acts 2, the early church didn't just gather on Sunday mornings. They were devoted to fellowship and breaking bread together "day by day" (Acts 2:46). They were living life together. We see this pattern all through Acts as the church grows and spreads. Believers intertwined their lives with one another: "Now the full number of those who believed were of one heart and soul . . . they had everything in common" (Acts 4:32). These members of the early church practiced hospitality, encouraged one another with the word, took care of the poor, supported missionaries, and spread the gospel. They were thriving!

One distinct mark of Jesus's disciples is that we love one another as he has loved us (John 13:34–35). This kind of love requires more than seeing each other just one day a week. The way to thrive in your local church is to intertwine your life with the lives of others in the church. Of course, this starts by consistently showing up on Sunday. But we continue fellowship throughout the week by making room in our hearts and homes for others.

Kate is a homeschooling mother of three young children, and she's pregnant with her fourth. She hosts a small group of adults in her home, leads a small group of teenage girls on another night, and invites women to come over during the week while she does chores.

Naomi, married to an unbeliever, regularly houses women from the church, teaches Scripture at a women's Bible study, and spends much of her time discipling young women.

Tala is an Egyptian student from a Muslim background. Even though her family abandoned her, she has found a new family in the church. She lives with church members, enthusiastically encourages others, and is surrounded by supportive sisters and brothers.

Adiam is a widow with three grown children who live in different parts of the world. She gives people rides to church, opens her home for hospitality, and partners with others in the church to share the gospel with her friends and neighbors.

Mary is a forty-something, single woman who works as an administrator. Severely abused as a child, she used to be a drug addict living in the cab of a truck. She now blesses others with her creative art and cooking, prays for missionaries supported by her church, and counsels teenagers and women of all ages.

These five women bring the church home with them. Their lives revolve around the people of God. They are all in various stages of life. They have different abilities and different struggles. Their trials are real. But Jesus has called these women to himself, and he has called them to his church, so even in their struggles they are thriving. Bring the church home with you, love others as Christ has loved you, and thrive.

Thriving Is a Community Project

Bookstores are brimming with books designed to help women. You'll find manuals for self-empowerment, "ten rules" for good relationships, or "twelve steps" to a good life. Exercise, eat right, drink green tea, do something enjoyable each day, wash your face: each of these recommendations is supposed to increase your overall sense of well-being. But sisters, the way for us to truly thrive is to build our lives around Jesus and the local church.

If you have believed the gospel, you are part of the beautiful bride of Christ. One day this bride will be presented to her groom adorned in splendor, radiant "like a most rare jewel, like a jasper, clear as crystal" (Rev. 21:11). Jesus treasures his bride, so much that he gave himself up for her. So also, let's treasure the church and make ourselves ready as we wait "for our blessed hope, the appearing of the glory of our great God and Savior Jesus Christ" (Titus 2:13).

Recommended Resource

Erin Wheeler, *The Good Portion: The Doctrine of the Church for Every Woman* (Ross-Shire, Scotland: Christian Focus, 2021).

Notes

1. Personal stories involving other individuals are shared in this booklet with permission from those individuals. Often pseudonyms have been used for privacy.
2. For more advice on how to get started in discipling relationships, check out Garrett Kell's booklet *How Can I Find Someone to Disciple Me?*, Church Questions (Wheaton, IL: Crossway, 2021).
3. "Welcome to the Spiritual Gifts Survey," Team Ministry website, accessed January 27, 2020, https://gifts.church growth.org/spiritual-gifts-survey/.
4. For more on how to serve your church faithfully and on how to think about gifts and service, see Matthew Emadi's booklet *How Can I Serve My Church?*, Church Questions (Wheaton, IL: Crossway, 2021).

Scripture Index

IX 9Marks

Building Healthy Churches

9Marks exists to equip church leaders with a biblical vision and practical resources for displaying God's glory to the nations through healthy churches.

To that end, we want to see churches characterized by these nine marks of health:

1. Expositional Preaching
2. Gospel Doctrine
3. A Biblical Understanding of Conversion and Evangelism
4. Biblical Church Membership
5. Biblical Church Discipline
6. A Biblical Concern for Discipleship and Growth
7. Biblical Church Leadership
8. A Biblical Understanding of the Practice of Prayer
9. A Biblical Understanding and Practice of Missions

Find all our Crossway titles and other resources at 9Marks.org.